★ ★ ★ ★ ★

THE COMPLETE BOOK OF

COCKTAILS

★ ★ ★ ★ ★

pil

Publications International, Ltd.

Let's get social!

 @Publications_International

@PublicationsInternational

www.pilcookbooks.com

CONTENTS

COCKTAIL BASICS

SETTING UP A BAR

When setting up a bar, keep it simple. You don't need a full bar that offers numerous mixed drinks, beer, and wine. The time and expense it would take to include every one of your guests' favorite beverages may be better spent in other ways. For a cocktail party, consider limiting the selection to a couple of popular mixed drinks, like martinis or margaritas. Then, add wine and beer, and most everyone will find something to their liking.

When serving alcohol, always make sure that there is a selection of non-alcoholic beverages as well. Water and soft drinks can be augmented by juice, punch, and iced tea.

COCKTAIL BASICS

Timeless and trendy? Yes! The wonderful world of cocktails combines the stylish classics that have been around for decades with fresh new twists that keep things exciting. You don't need to immerse yourself in cocktail culture to enjoy it, but some basic bar knowledge will make creating great cocktails easy—and fun!

Start with the fundamentals, such as getting the right tools and stocking the bar. The following pages will show you what you'll need to prepare the recipes in this book.

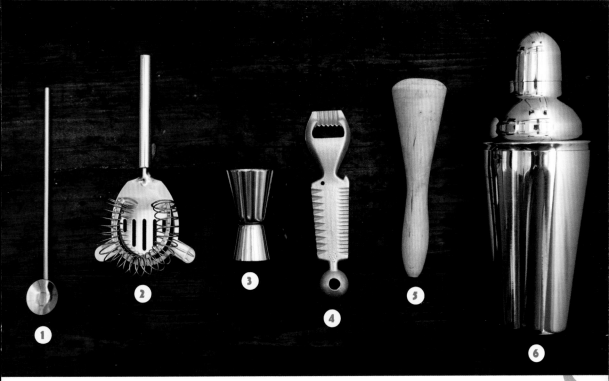

BAR TOOLS

BAR SPOON (1): A long-handled metal spoon to stir drinks in a mixing glass or other tall glass.

BLENDER: A necessary tool for making ice cream drinks and slushy drinks like frozen daiquiris or smoothies. Also useful for crushing ice.

CHANNEL KNIFE (4): An inexpensive tool with a metal tooth for peeling long thin twists from citrus fruit for garnishing.

CITRUS JUICER: Can be anything from a simple wooden reamer or metal press to a fancy electric juicer.

CORKSCREW: A waiter's corkscrew is a popular style which includes a small blade to cut the from wine caps as well as a bottle opener.

JIGGER (3): A two-sided stainless steel measuring tool, preferably with 1- and 1½-ounce cups.

MIXING GLASS: A large glass (at least 16 ounces) used for shaking or stirring drinks with ice to chill them.

COCKTAILS BASICS

★ ★ ★ ★ ★

MUDDLER (5): A long, sturdy tool—usually made of wood—used to crush ingredients like herbs, fresh fruit, and sugar.

SHAKER (6): A standard metal cocktail shaker is the most common style, which includes the container, a lid with a built-in strainer and a cap for the lid.

STRAINER (2): To mix drinks in a mixing glass, a Hawthorne bar strainer—flat with a spring coil around its edge—is necessary to keep the ice and muddled fruit out of your drinks.

OTHER TOOLS FROM YOUR KITCHEN THAT ARE ALSO USEFUL AT THE BAR:

- Cutting board
- Measuring spoons
- Paring knife

- Pitcher
- Tongs
- Vegetable peeler

COCKTAIL BASICS

★ ★ ★ ★ ★

GLASSWARE

Don't worry—you don't need all of these glasses in your home bar!
Think about what you like to drink and what you typically serve
to guests, then purchase accordingly. (Some of them can do double
duty.)

CHAMPAGNE FLUTE
4 to 10 ounces

COCKTAIL (also called a martini glass)
3 to 10 ounces

COLLINS
12 to 14 ounces, taller and narrower than a
highball glass, often used for drinks served
over ice

COUPE
Shallow with a wide mouth

HIGHBALL
10 to 12 ounces, tall and narrow to preserve
the fizz in drinks with tonic or soda water

COCKTAILS BASICS

★ ★ ★ ★ ★

HURRICANE
12 to 16 ounces, shaped like a hurricane lamp and used for hurricanes and other tropical drinks

MARGARITA
12 to 14 ounces, used for margaritas and daiquiris

OLD FASHIONED (also called a rocks glass)
4 to 8 ounces, short and wide-mouthed for spirits served neat or drinks served over ice (double old fashioned glasses hold 12 to 16 ounces)

PILSNER GLASS
Tall, thin, flared glass used for beer or oversized drinks

SHOT GLASS
1 to 3 ounces, used for shooters and for measuring

WHITE WINE
6 to 12 ounces

RED WINE
8 to 24 ounces

COCKTAIL BASICS

★ ★ ★ ★ ★

STOCKING THE BAR

Buy what you like and what you'll use most often. The better the ingredients, the better your drinks will be. (But keep in mind that the most expensive ingredients aren't always the best ones.)

SPIRITS	MIXERS
• Brandy	• Citrus juices (fresh lemon, lime and orange)
• Champagne or other sparkling wine	• Club soda
• Gin	• Cola
• Liqueurs (almond, coffee, maraschino and orange flavors are some of the most common)	• Ginger ale
	• Lemon-lime soda
	• Tomato juice (plain or spicy)
• Rum	• Tonic water
• Tequila	• Water (plain or sparkling)
• Vodka	• Whipping cream
• Whiskey (bourbon, Scotch, etc.)	
• Wine (including fortified wines like port, sherry and vermouth)	

COCKTAILS BASICS

★ ★ ★ ★ ★

FLAVORINGS	GARNISHES
• Bitters	• Celery
• Grenadine	• Lemons
• Hot pepper sauce	• Limes
• Salt (coarse)	• Maraschino cherries
• Sugar (granulated and superfine or powdered)	• Mint sprigs
• Worcestershire sauce	• Olives
	• Oranges

COCKTAIL BASICS

★ ★ ★ ★ ★

SERVING AND GARNISHING

Cocktails should be served immediately after preparing them for the best flavor and texture, so you should have all glassware chilled and garnishes ready before you begin mixing. Enjoy preparing your cocktails while choosing from a wide collection of glassware, colored straws, stirrers, and garnishes to make them fun and appealing. The simple ideas below are just a few of the many ways to garnish a cocktail.

Recipe Ingredients

For a simple garnish, choose an ingredient like a strawberry, cherry, orange, lemon, lime, or an herb. Place it on the rim of the glass or float it on top of the cocktail. Small pieces of fruit or olives on toothpicks also make attractive garnishes.

Fruit and Chocolate Curls

Use a citrus peeler to easily create fruit and chocolate curls. When making a fruit curl, be careful to remove only the colored part of the peel with the citrus peeler, not the bitter white pith. The peel may then be cut into thinner strips, if desired. Twist the strips around straws and then place the straws in ice water in the refrigerator to set the curl.

For chocolate curls, place one 1-ounce square of semisweet chocolate on a microwavable plate and microwave on HIGH 5 to 10 seconds. (Chocolate should still be firm.) Pull the citrus peeler across the chocolate to create curls. Place on a waxed paper-lined baking sheet and refrigerate 15 minutes or until firm.

Glassware Rims

Glassware rims can be coated with salt, sugar, coconut or even graham cracker crumbs. To create extra-fine coatings, place in a blender and pulse until the desired texture is reached. Place coatings in small bowls that fit the entire rim of the glass. Wet rims with water or fruit juice, then dip in desired coatings.

COCKTAILS BASICS

SEASONAL CELEBRATIONS

While many drinks are year-round classics, cocktails, just like cooking, can change with the seasons.

SPRING: Stir up simple, cool refreshing drinks such as Pimm's Cup (*page 52*) or Buck's Fizz (*page 126*).

SUMMER: Try fresh, fruity, thirst-quenching drinks like Shandy (*page 114*) or Aperol Spritz (*page 128*).

FALL: Drinks with intense autumn flavors, colors, and spices take center stage, like Stone Fence (*page 122*), Manzarita (*page 80*), and Cider Sangria (*page 120*).

WINTER: Serve fun and festive drinks to toast the holidays, such as a Pomegranate Mimosa (*page 126*) or Cranberry Caipirinha (*page 142*). Or, warm up your guests with hot drinks like a Hot Mulled Cider (*page 154*) or a Hot Toddy (*page 96*).

TIPS AND TRICKS

• Use fresh fruit juices for the best drinks. If you can't squeeze your own, try to purchase fresh juice from the store. And always wash your citrus fruits before juicing them or making garnishes.

• Chilled glasses keep your cocktails cool much longer than room-temperature glasses. To chill glasses, put them in the freezer for 30 minutes or in the refrigerator for several hours before preparing your drinks. Or, you can fill a glass with crushed ice and let it stand while you mix the drink. Dump out the ice when you're ready to pour the drink.

• Make sure your mixers are cold! When you've gone to the trouble of chilling your glasses, you don't want to warm up your cocktails with room temperature mixers.

COCKTAIL BASICS

★ ★ ★ ★ ★

- Many recipes call for filling a cocktail shaker with ice—the ice should fill the shaker half to two-thirds full. Usually the ice is added first so it chills the shaker and ingredients as they're added.

- Pour a cocktail from the shaker or mixing glass immediately after shaking or stirring—letting it stand will dilute the drink.

- Drinks with egg whites, such as Ramos Gin Fizz (*page 52*), need to be shaken extra vigorously to incorporate the egg white. Use the freshest eggs possible, or you can use pasteurized eggs. (Do not use egg substitutes.)

- When serving hot drinks, make sure the glasses or cups are made of heatproof glass.

CONVERSION CHART

¼ ounce = ½ tablespoon	6 ounces = ¾ cup
½ ounce = 1 tablespoon	8 ounces = 1 cup
¾ ounce = 1½ tablespoons	16 ounces = 2 cups
1 ounce = 2 tablespoons	24 ounces = 3 cups
2 ounces = ¼ cup	32 ounces = 1 quart
4 ounces = ½ cup	

★ ★ ★ ★ ★

RUM

★ ★ ★ ★ ★

Rum is made from sugar cane or its by-products such as syrup, molasses, and juice. It can be classified into one or more categories including white or clear rum, gold rum, dark rum, or black rum.

- White or clear rum has a mild flavor and is lighter in body than gold or dark rums. It is most commonly used to create cocktails.

- Gold rum takes on a gold or amber hue after mellowing in a barrel over time. Flavors like vanilla, almond, citrus, caramel, or coconut may be present from the type of barrels used. Coloring may also be added to provide consistency.

- Dark rum is most commonly aged in oak barrels for two or more years. It develops a richer flavor and takes on hues of mahogany, copper, and caramel.

- Black rum is the richest, darkest, and heaviest-bodied rum. It retains most of the rich sugar cane molasses and caramel flavoring during distilling. The barrels used to mature it are fired heavily or charred, giving the rum its strong flavor.

◀ Mojito *(page 16)*

CUBA LIBRE ▶
MAKES 1 SERVING

2 ounces rum
Chilled cola
Lime wedge

Fill chilled highball glass half full with ice. Pour rum over ice; fill with cola. Garnish with lime wedge.

MOJITO
MAKES 2 SERVINGS

8 fresh mint leaves, plus additional for garnish

12 ounces lime juice

2 teaspoons superfine sugar or powdered sugar

3 ounces light rum

Soda water

2 lime slices

Combine half of mint leaves, lime juice and sugar in each of two highball glasses; mash with wooden spoon or muddler. Fill glass with ice. Pour rum over ice; top with soda water. Garnish with lime slices and mint sprigs.

DAIQUIRI ▶
MAKES 1 SERVING

1½ ounces light rum

¾ ounce lime juice

¼ ounce simple syrup
(recipe follows)
or 1 teaspoon
powdered sugar

Lime wedge

Fill cocktail shaker half full with ice; add rum, lime juice and simple syrup. Shake until blended; strain into chilled cocktail glass or margarita glass. Garnish with lime wedge.

SIMPLE SYRUP

Bring 1 cup water to a boil; stir in 1 cup sugar. Reduce heat to low; stir constantly until sugar is dissolved. Cool to room temperature; store syrup in glass jar in refrigerator.

PALMETTO
MAKES 1 SERVING

1½ ounces light rum

1 ounce sweet
vermouth

2 dashes orange
bitters

Lemon twist

Fill cocktail shaker half full with ice; add rum, vermouth and bitters. Shake until blended; strain into chilled cocktail glass. Garnish with lemon twist.

PLANTER'S PUNCH ▸
MAKES 1 SERVING

3 ounces orange juice

2 ounces dark rum

Juice of ½ lime

2 teaspoons powdered sugar

¼ teaspoon grenadine

Orange slices and fresh strawberry

Fill cocktail shaker half full with ice; add orange juice, rum, lime juice, sugar and grenadine. Shake until blended; strain into chilled ice-filled glass. Garnish with orange slices and strawberry.

COCO LOCO
MAKES 1 SERVING

4 ounces pineapple juice

2 ounces light rum

1 ounce cream of coconut

1 ounce milk

½ ounce amaretto

1 teaspoon grenadine

½ cup ice cubes

Pineapple wedge and/ or maraschino cherry

Combine pineapple juice, rum, cream of coconut, milk, amaretto, grenadine and ice in blender; blend until smooth. Serve in wine glass or hollowed-out coconut. Garnish with pineapple wedge.

DARK AND STORMY ▶
MAKES 1 SERVING

4 ounces ginger beer

2 ounces dark rum

½ ounce lime juice

Fill old fashioned or Collins glass with ice. Add ginger beer, rum and lime juice; stir until blended.

ZOMBIE
MAKES 1 SERVING

2 ounces light rum

1 ounce dark rum

1 ounce lime juice

1 ounce pineapple juice

1 ounce orange juice or papaya juice

½ ounce apricot brandy

1 teaspoon sugar

½ cup crushed ice

½ ounce 151-proof rum

½ ounce grenadine

Pineapple spear, orange slice and maraschino cherry

Fresh mint sprig

Combine light rum, dark rum, lime juice, pineapple juice, orange juice, brandy, sugar and ice in blender; blend until smooth. Pour mixture into chilled Collins or highball glass. Float 151-proof rum and grenadine on top. Garnish with pineapple spear, orange slice, maraschino cherry and mint.

VARIATION

Fill cocktail shaker half full with ice; add all ingredients except crushed ice, 151-proof rum, grenadine and garnishes. Shake until blended; strain into chilled Collins glass. Float 151-proof rum and grenadine on top. Garnish with pineapple spear, orange slice, maraschino cherry and mint.

RUM SWIZZLE
MAKES 1 SERVING

2 ounces rum

1 ounce lime juice

1 teaspoon superfine sugar

2 dashes Angostura bitters

Lime slice

Combine rum, lime juice, sugar and bitters in chilled Collins or highball glass filled with crushed ice; stir vigorously with long spoon until blended. Garnish with lime slice.

NOTE

Swizzles originated in the Caribbean in the early 1800's. These tall rum drinks were served over crushed ice and mixed with long twigs; the twigs were rubbed rapidly between one's hands, which was called "swizzling." Most swizzle drinks today are mixed with long bar spoons and they can contain spirits other than rum.

BEACHCOMBER ▶
MAKES 1 SERVING

2 ounces light rum	Fill cocktail shaker with ice; add rum, orange liqueur, lime juice and maraschino liqueur. Shake until blended; strain into chilled cocktail glass. Garnish with maraschino cherry.
1 ounce orange liqueur	
1 ounce lime juice	
¼ ounce maraschino liqueur	
Maraschino cherry	

EL PRESIDENTE
MAKES 1 SERVING

1½ ounces white rum	Fill cocktail shaker half full with ice; add rum, vermouth, liqueur and grenadine. Shake about 25 seconds or until cold; strain into chilled cocktail glass. Garnish with orange twist.
¾ ounce dry vermouth	
½ ounce orange liqueur	
½ teaspoon grenadine	
Orange twist	

JUNGLE BIRD ▶
MAKES 1 SERVING

1½ ounces Jamaican or dark aged rum

1½ ounces pineapple juice

¾ ounce Campari

½ ounce lime juice

½ ounce simple syrup (recipe follows)

Pineapple wedge

Fill cocktail shaker with ice; add rum, pineapple juice, Campari, lime juice and simple syrup. Shake 30 seconds or until cold; strain into ice-filled old fashioned glass, copper mug or tiki mug. Garnish with pineapple wedge.

SIMPLE SYRUP

Bring 1 cup water to a boil; stir in 1 cup sugar. Reduce heat to low; stir constantly until sugar is dissolved. Cool to room temperature; store syrup in glass jar in refrigerator.

GROG
MAKES 1 SERVING

2 ounces dark rum

½ ounce lemon juice

1 teaspoon packed brown sugar

2 to 3 whole cloves

¾ cup boiling water

1 cinnamon stick

Combine rum, lemon juice, brown sugar and cloves in warm mug. Pour in boiling water; stir with cinnamon stick until brown sugar is dissolved.

RUM

★ ★ ★ ★ ★

HAVANA SPECIAL ▶
MAKES 1 SERVING

2 ounces pineapple juice

1½ ounces light rum

¼ ounce maraschino liqueur

Fill cocktail shaker half full with ice; add pineapple juice, rum and liqueur. Shake until blended; strain into ice-filled highball glass or cocktail glass.

MAI TAI
MAKES 1 SERVING

1 ounce light rum

1 ounce triple sec

½ ounce grenadine

½ ounce orgeat syrup*

½ ounce fresh lime juice

1 ounce dark rum

Pineapple wedge and maraschino cherry

*Almond-flavored syrup.

Fill cocktail shaker half full with ice; add light rum, triple sec, grenadine, orgeat syrup and lime juice. Shake until blended; strain into chilled cocktail glass. Pour dark rum over top; do not stir. Garnish with pineapple and maraschino cherry; serve with straw.

PIÑA COLADA
MAKES 1 SERVING

4 ounces pineapple juice (½ cup)

1½ ounces light rum

1½ ounces coconut cream

½ cup crushed ice

Pineapple wedge and maraschino cherry

Combine pineapple juice, rum and coconut cream in blender. Add ice; blend 15 seconds or until smooth. Pour into glass; garnish with pineapple and maraschino cherry.

PIÑITA COLADA

Omit rum.

KIWI COLADA

Peel, halve and seed 1 kiwi. Add to blender with ice; blend 15 seconds or until smooth. Pour into cocktail glass; garnish with kiwi slice, lemon peel and mint sprig.

FROZEN DAIQUIRI ▶
MAKES 1 SERVING

1½ ounces light rum

1½ ounces lime juice

½ ounce triple sec

1 teaspoon sugar or simple syrup

1 cup crushed ice

Lime twist (optional)

Strawberry halves (optional)

Place rum, lime juice, triple sec and sugar in blender. Add ice; blend 15 seconds or until smooth. Pour into glass; garnish with lime twist and strawberry halves.

FROZEN STRAWBERRY DAIQUIRI (pictured)

Add 4 to 5 chopped strawberries and ¼ ounce strawberry liqueur to blender with ice. Garnish with strawberry.

BLUE HAWAIIAN
MAKES 1 SERVING

1 ounce light rum

½ ounce blue curaçao

1 ounce pineapple juice

1 ounce cream of coconut

1 teaspoon sugar

Strawberry and pineapple slice

Fill cocktail shaker half full with ice; add rum, curaçao, pineapple juice, cream of coconut and sugar. Shake until blended; strain into ice-filled old fashioned glass. Garnish with strawberry and pineapple.

LONG ISLAND ICED TEA ▶
MAKES 1 SERVING

½ ounce light rum

½ ounce tequila

½ ounce vodka

½ ounce gin

½ ounce triple sec

1 ounce lemon juice

1 teaspoon sugar or simple syrup

Chilled cola

Lemon wedge and maraschino cherry

Fill cocktail shaker half full with ice; add rum, tequila, vodka, gin, triple sec, lemon juice and sugar. Shake until blended; strain into ice-filled highball glass. Fill with cola; garnish with lemon wedge and maraschino cherry.

HURRICANE
MAKES 1 SERVING

2 ounces light rum

2 ounces dark rum

1 ounce passion fruit juice

1 ounce orange juice

1 ounce lime juice

½ ounce grenadine (optional)

Pineapple wedges and maraschino cherry

Fill cocktail shaker half full with ice; add rum, juices and grenadine, if desired. Shake until blended; strain into ice-filled glass. Garnish with pineapple and maraschino cherry.

GIN

The name "gin" is derived from the French word "genièvre," the Dutch word "jenever" and the Italian word "ginepro," meaning "juniper." This pale yellow liquor is the purified spirits from a grain mash, then flavored with the juniper berry. There are four varieties of gin including London dry, Plymouth, old Tom, and Dutch.

- London dry gin has dried lemon and/or orange peels added to it, which gives it a citrus flavor and aroma.

- Plymouth gin is slightly less dry than London dry gin. It has a more earthy flavor that softens the juniper flavor.

- Old Tom is called the "missing link" between the malty Dutch gin and the sharp-edged London dry gin. Its sweetness comes from naturally sweet botanicals, malts, and/or added sugar.

- Dutch gin, also called Belgian gin, comes from distilling malt wine.

◀ Gin Sour (page 40)

GIN

★ ★ ★ ★ ★

CLOVER CLUB ▶
MAKES 1 SERVING

1½ ounces gin
¾ ounce lemon juice
½ ounce dry vermouth
2 teaspoons grenadine
  or raspberry syrup
1 egg white

Combine gin, lemon juice, vermouth, grenadine and egg white in cocktail shaker; shake 10 seconds without ice. Fill shaker with ice; shake about 30 seconds or until cold and frothy. Strain into chilled cocktail glass.

GIN SOUR
MAKES 1 SERVING

2 ounces gin
¾ ounce lemon juice
¾ ounce simple syrup
  (recipe follows)
Lemon twist

Fill cocktail shaker with ice; add gin, lemon juice and simple syrup. Shake until blended; strain into chilled cocktail glass or coupe. Garnish with lemon twist.

FITZGERALD
Add 2 dashes Angostura bitters to cocktail shaker; proceed as directed.

SIMPLE SYRUP
Bring 1 cup water to a boil; stir in 1 cup sugar. Reduce heat to low; stir constantly until sugar is dissolved. Cool to room temperature; store syrup in glass jar in refrigerator.

GIN

★　★　★　★　★

FRENCH 75 ▶
MAKES 1 SERVING

- 2 ounces gin
- ½ ounce lemon juice
- 1 teaspoon superfine sugar
- 2 ounces chilled champagne or sparkling wine

Fill cocktail shaker with ice; add gin, lemon juice and sugar. Shake about 15 seconds or until cold; strain into champagne flute or coupe. Top with champagne; stir gently.

LIME RICKEY
MAKES 1 SERVING

- 2 ounces gin
- 2 ounces vodka
- 2 ounces lime juice
- Club soda
- Lime wedge

Fill cocktail glass with ice; pour gin, vodka and lime juice over ice. Top with club soda to fill. Garnish with lime wedge.

RASPBERRY RICKEY

Place ⅓ cup raspberries in small bowl; sprinkle with 2 teaspoons sugar. Add lime juice; let sit 10 minutes. Press through sieve to remove seeds. Combine raspberry mixture, 2 ounces raspberry-flavored vodka and 2 ounces gin in ice-filled old fashioned glass. Fill with club soda. Garnish with fresh raspberries and mint leaves.

GIN ST. CLEMENT'S ▸
MAKES 1 SERVING

1½ ounces gin

1 ounce lemon juice

1 ounce orange juice

2 ounces tonic water

Orange and/or
lemon slices

Fill Collins or highball glass with ice; add gin, lemon juice and orange juice. Top with tonic water; stir until blended. Garnish with orange slice.

GIMLET
MAKES 1 SERVING

2 ounces gin

1 ounce lime juice

1 ounce simple syrup
(recipe follows)

Lime wedge

Fill cocktail shaker half full with ice; add gin, lime juice and simple syrup. Shake until blended; strain into chilled martini glass. Garnish with lime wedge.

SIMPLE SYRUP

Bring 1 cup water to a boil; stir in 1 cup sugar. Reduce heat to low; stir constantly until sugar is dissolved. Cool to room temperature; store syrup in glass jar in refrigerator.

MARTINEZ ▶
MAKES 1 SERVING

1½ ounces gin

¾ ounce sweet vermouth

½ ounce maraschino liqueur

2 dashes orange bitters

Lemon or orange twist

Fill mixing glass with ice; add gin, vermouth, liqueur and bitters. Stir about 20 seconds or until very cold; strain into chilled coupe or cocktail glass. Garnish with lemon twist.

GIN AND TONIC
MAKES 1 SERVING

2 ounces gin

4 ounces tonic water

Green grape (optional)

Lime wedge (optional)

Fill old fashioned glass with ice; pour gin over ice. Stir in tonic water. Garnish with grape and lime wedge.

SOUTH SIDE ▶
MAKES 1 SERVING

2 ounces gin

¾ ounce lemon juice

¾ ounce simple syrup
(recipe follows)

5 fresh mint leaves

Fresh mint sprig
and/or lemon
twist

Fill cocktail shaker with ice; add gin, lemon juice, simple syrup and mint leaves. Shake until blended; strain into ice-filled Collins glass or chilled cocktail glass. Garnish with mint sprig and/or lemon twist.

SIMPLE SYRUP

Bring 1 cup water to a boil; stir in 1 cup sugar. Reduce heat to low; stir constantly until sugar is dissolved. Cool to room temperature; store syrup in glass jar in refrigerator.

BRONX
MAKES 1 SERVING

2 ounces gin

1 ounce orange juice

½ ounce dry
vermouth

½ ounce sweet
vermouth

Orange twist or
slice

Fill cocktail shaker with ice; add gin, orange juice, dry vermouth and sweet vermouth. Shake until blended; strain into chilled cocktail glass. Garnish with orange twist.

TUXEDO COCKTAIL ▶

MAKES 1 SERVING

1½ ounces gin

1 ounce dry vermouth

½ teaspoon maraschino liqueur

¼ teaspoon absinthe or Pernod

2 dashes orange bitters

Maraschino cherry

Fill mixing glass or cocktail shaker with ice; add gin, vermouth, liqueur, absinthe and bitters. Stir until very cold; strain into chilled cocktail glass. Garnish with maraschino cherry.

VESPER

MAKES 1 SERVING

3 ounces gin

1 ounce vodka

½ ounce Lillet Blanc

Lemon twist

Fill cocktail shaker with ice; add gin, vodka and Lillet Blanc. Shake until blended; strain into chilled cocktail glass. Garnish with lemon twist.

RAMOS GIN FIZZ ▶

MAKES 1 SERVING

2 ounces gin

1 ounce whipping cream

½ ounce lemon juice

½ ounce lime juice

1 teaspoon superfine sugar

2 dashes orange flower water

1 egg white

Chilled club soda

Combine gin, cream, lemon juice, lime juice, sugar, orange flower water and egg white in cocktail shaker; shake without ice 30 seconds. Add 1 cup ice to shaker; shake about 20 seconds or until cold. Strain into highball or Collins glass; top with club soda.

NOTE

A Ramos Gin Fizz is typically not served over ice, but if you don't have a chilled glass, adding a few ice cubes will help keep the drink cold longer (although it will also dilute the drink).

PIMM'S CUP

MAKES 1 SERVING

2 ounces Pimm's No. 1

Lemon-lime soda

Cucumber strip or spear

Lemon twist

Fill chilled highball glass with ice; pour in Pimm's. Top with lemon-lime soda; garnish with cucumber and lemon twist.

GIN

★ ★ ★ ★ ★

NEGRONI ▶
MAKES 1 SERVING

1 ounce gin

1 ounce Campari

1 ounce sweet or dry vermouth

Orange slice or twist

Fill cocktail shaker half full with ice; add gin, Campari and vermouth. Stir until blended; strain into chilled cocktail glass. Garnish with orange slice.

BUCK
MAKES 1 SERVING

Juice of ¼ lime

1½ ounces gin

Ginger ale

Lemon slice

Fill old fashioned glass with ice; squeeze lime juice over ice and drop lime into glass. Add gin and ginger ale to fill; stir gently. Garnish with lemon slice.

TOM COLLINS ▶
MAKES 1 SERVING

2 ounces gin

1 ounce lemon juice

1 teaspoon superfine sugar

3 ounces chilled club soda

Lemon slice

Fill cocktail shaker half full with ice; add gin, lemon juice and sugar. Shake until blended; strain into ice-filled Collins glass. Fill with club soda. Garnish with lemon slice.

SINGAPORE SLING
MAKES 1 SERVING

1 ounce gin

½ ounce lime juice

½ ounce cherry liqueur

¼ ounce orange liqueur

¼ ounce Bénédictine

1 tablespoon grenadine

4 ounces pineapple juice

Dash of bitters

Maraschino cherry and pineapple wedge

Fill cocktail shaker half full with ice; add all ingredients except garnishes. Shake until blended; strain into ice-filled highball glass. Garnish with maraschino cherry and pineapple.

★ ★ ★ ★ ★

VODKA

★ ★ ★ ★ ★

Vodka's base can be made from grains, potatoes, wheat, corn, or fruit. Different countries use different bases or ingredients for its production. There are basically two types of vodkas—flavored and non-flavored.

- Flavored vodka has a recognizable smell and flavor. The most popular flavors include apple, berries, cherries, peaches, honey, coffee, pepper, citrus, and chocolate.

- Non-flavored vodka simply has no recognizable smell or flavor. Even though it is not flavored, the base ingredient can still be recognized.

◄ Cosmopolitan (page 60)

VODKA MARTINI ▶
MAKES 1 SERVING

2 ounces vodka or gin

½ ounce dry vermouth

Fill cocktail shaker half full with ice; add vodka and vermouth. Stir or shake until blended; strain into chilled cocktail glass.

DIRTY MARTINI (pictured)

Add 1 to 2 teaspoons olive brine to Martini or Classic Dry Martini; garnish with olives.

GIBSON

Garnish Martini or Classic Dry Martini with cocktail onion.

COSMOPOLITAN
MAKES 1 SERVING

2 ounces vodka or lemon-flavored vodka

1 ounce triple sec

1 ounce cranberry juice

½ ounce lime juice

Lime wedge

Fill cocktail shaker half full with ice; add vodka, triple sec and juices. Shake until blended; strain into chilled cocktail glass. Garnish with lime wedge.

MOSCOW MULE ▶
MAKES 1 SERVING

½ lime, cut into
  2 wedges

1½ ounces vodka

4 to 6 ounces chilled
  ginger beer

Lime slices and
  fresh mint sprigs

Fill copper mug or Collins glass half full with ice. Squeeze lime juice over ice; drop wedges into mug. Pour vodka over ice; top with ginger beer. Garnish with lime slices and mint.

BLOODY BULL
MAKES 1 SERVING

3 ounces tomato
  juice or spicy
  vegetable juice

2 ounces vodka

2 ounces beef
  bouillon granules

½ ounce lemon juice

¼ teaspoon
  Worcestershire
  sauce

Dash hot pepper
  sauce

Salt and black
  pepper

Cherry tomato or
  lemon wedge

Fill cocktail shaker two thirds full with ice; add tomato juice, vodka, bouillon, lemon juice, Worcestershire sauce, hot pepper sauce and salt and black pepper. Shake until blended; strain into ice-filled highball glass. Garnish with cherry tomato.

CHERRY COLLINS ▶

MAKES 1 SERVING

2 ounces cherry-
  flavored vodka

¾ ounce lemon juice

¾ simple syrup
  (recipe follows)

Club soda

Fresh cherries

Fill highball glass with ice; add vodka, lemon juice and simple syrup. Stir until blended; top with club soda. Garnish with cherries.

SIMPLE SYRUP

Bring 1 cup water to a boil; stir in 1 cup sugar. Reduce heat to low; stir constantly until sugar is dissolved. Cool to room temperature; store syrup in glass jar in refrigerator.

FRENCH MARTINI

MAKES 1 SERVING

2 ounces vodka

2 ounces pineapple
  juice

½ ounce raspberry
  liqueur

Fill cocktail shaker with ice; add vodka, pineapple juice and liqueur. Shake until blended; strain into chilled cocktail glass.

WEST SIDE ▶
MAKES 1 SERVING

2 ounces lemon-flavored vodka

1 ounce lemon juice

½ ounce simple syrup (recipe follows)

1 sprig fresh mint

Chilled club soda

Fill cocktail shaker with ice; add vodka, lemon juice, simple syrup and mint. Shake until blended. Top with splash of club soda; strain into chilled coupe or cocktail glass.

SIMPLE SYRUP

Bring 1 cup water to a boil; stir in 1 cup sugar. Reduce heat to low; stir constantly until sugar is dissolved. Cool to room temperature; store syrup in glass jar in refrigerator.

MADRAS
MAKES 1 SERVING

3 ounces cranberry juice

2 ounces vodka

1½ ounces orange juice

Lime slices or wedges

Combine cranberry juice, vodka and orange juice in ice-filled highball or Collins glass; stir until blended. Garnish with lime slices.

BLOODY MARY ▶

MAKES 1 SERVING

Dash *each* Worcestershire sauce, hot pepper sauce, celery salt, black pepper and salt

3 ounces tomato juice

1½ ounces vodka

½ ounce lemon juice

Celery stalk with leaves, pickle spear, lemon slice and/or green olives

Fill highball glass with ice; add dashes of Worcestershire sauce, hot pepper sauce, celery salt, black pepper and salt. Add tomato juice, vodka and lemon juice; stir gently until blended. Serve with desired garnishes.

VODKA SUNRISE

MAKES 1 SERVING

5 ounces orange juice

1 ounce vodka

½ ounce grenadine

Orange slice

Fill highball glass half full with ice; add orange juice and vodka. Stir until blended; top with grenadine. Garnish with orange slice.

LEMON DROP ▶
MAKES 1 SERVING

1 teaspoon sugar
  (optional)

2 ounces vodka

¾ ounce lemon juice
  (about ½ lemon)

½ ounce simple syrup
  (recipe follows)

Lemon slice

Moisten rim of chilled shot or martini glass; dip in sugar, if desired. Place ice cubes in cocktail shaker; add vodka, lemon juice and simple syrup. Shake until blended; strain into glass. Garnish with lemon slice.

SIMPLE SYRUP

Bring 1 cup water to a boil; stir in 1 cup sugar. Reduce heat to low; stir constantly until sugar is dissolved. Cool to room temperature; store syrup in glass jar in refrigerator.

SALTY DOG
MAKES 1 SERVING

6 ounces grapefruit
  juice (¾ cup)

Salt

1½ ounces vodka

Moisten rim of cocktail glass with grapefruit juice; dip in salt. Fill glass with ice; pour vodka over ice. Stir in grapefruit juice.

GREYHOUND

Omit salt.

BLACK RUSSIAN ▶
MAKES 1 SERVING

2 ounces vodka

1 ounce coffee
liqueur

Fill cocktail glass with ice. Add vodka and liqueur; stir.

WHITE RUSSIAN

Float 1 tablespoon cream over top of Black Russian.

SEA BREEZE
MAKES 1 SERVING

3 ounces cranberry
juice

2 ounces grapefruit
juice

1½ ounces vodka

Lemon slice

Fill cocktail shaker half full with ice; add cranberry juice, grapefruit juice and vodka. Shake until blended; strain into ice-filled Collins or highball glass. Garnish with lemon slice.

ELECTRIC LEMONADE ▸

MAKES 1 SERVING

2 ounces sweet and
  sour mix

1½ ounces vodka

½ ounce blue curaçao

Lemon-lime soda

Lime wedges

Fill Collins glass half full with ice; add sweet and sour mix, vodka and curaçao. Fill with soda. Garnish with lime wedges.

HARVEY WALLBANGER

MAKES 1 SERVING

3 ounces vodka

6 ounces orange juice
  (¾ cup)

1 ounce Galliano

Orange slice

Fill highball glass half full with ice; pour vodka over ice. Stir in orange juice. Pour Galliano over top; do not stir. Garnish with orange juice.

APPLE MARTINI ▶

MAKES 1 SERVING

2 ounces vodka

1 ounce apple schnapps

1 ounce apple juice

Apple or orange slice

Fill cocktail shaker half full with ice; add vodka, schnapps and apple juice. Shake until blended; strain into chilled martini glass. Garnish as desired.

SOUR APPLE MARTINI

Substitute sour apple schnapps for apple schnapps. Garnish with Granny Smith apple slice.

FUZZY NAVEL

MAKES 1 SERVING

4 ounces orange juice

1½ ounces peach schnapps

1 ounce vodka

Orange slice

Fill cocktail shaker half full with ice; add orange juice, schnapps and vodka. Shake until blended; strain into ice-filled glass. Garnish with orange slice.

★ ★ ★ ★ ★

TEQUILA

★ ★ ★ ★ ★

Tequila is made from the fermented sap of a blue agave plant. It can be classified into five categories: blanco, joven, reposado, añejo, and extra añejo.

- Blanco ("white") or plata ("silver") tequila is a white spirit that is unaged, bottled, and stored immediately after distillation.

- Joven ("young") or oro ("gold") tequila is unaged silver tequila that has been flavored with caramel coloring, oak extract, glycerin, or a sugar-based syrup.

- Reposado ("rested") tequila is aged a minimum of two months, but less than a year in any size oak barrel.

- Añejo ("aged" or "vintage") tequila is aged in small oak barrels for a minimum of one year, but less than three years.

- Extra añejo ("extra aged" or "ultra aged") tequila is aged a minimum of three years in oak barrels.

◄ Eldorado (page 80)

MANZARITA ▶
MAKES 1 SERVING

2 lemon quarters	Muddle lemon quarters and cinnamon in cocktail shaker. Fill shaker half full with ice; add tequila, cider and liqueur. Shake until blended; strain into ice-filled old fashioned glass. Garnish with cinnamon stick.
⅛ teaspoon ground cinnamon	
2 ounces tequila blanco (white or silver)	
1½ ounces apple cider (nonalcoholic)	
¾ ounce elderflower liqueur	
Cinnamon stick	

ELDORADO
MAKES 1 SERVING

2 ounces tequila	Fill cocktail shaker half full with ice; add tequila, honey and lemon juice. Shake until blended; strain into ice-filled old fashioned or Collins glass. Garnish with lemon slice.
1 tablespoon honey	
1½ ounces lemon juice	
Lemon or orange slice	

CLASSIC MARGARITA ▶

MAKES 2 SERVINGS

Lime wedges

Coarse salt

Ice

4 ounces tequila

2 ounces triple sec

2 ounces lime or
lemon juice

Additional lime
wedges

1. Rub rim of margarita glasses with lime wedges; dip in salt.

2. Fill cocktail shaker with ice; add tequila, triple sec and lime juice. Shake until blended; strain into glasses. Garnish with lime wedges.

FROZEN MARGARITA

Rub rim of margarita glasses with lime wedges; dip in salt. Combine tequila, triple sec, lime juice and 2 cups ice in blender; blend until smooth. Pour into prepared glasses; garnish with lime wedges. Makes 2 servings.

FROZEN STRAWBERRY MARGARITA

Rub rim of margarita glasses with lime wedges; dip in salt. Combine tequila, triple sec, lime juice, 1 cup frozen strawberries and 1 cup ice in blender; blend until smooth. Pour into prepared glasses; garnish with lime wedges and strawberries. Makes 2 servings.

BRAVE BULL ▶
MAKES 1 SERVING

1½ ounces tequila

1 ounce coffee liqueur

Lemon twist

Fill chilled old fashioned glass with ice; add tequila and liqueur. Stir until blended; garnish with lemon twist.

MEXICOLA
MAKES 1 SERVING

2 ounces tequila

½ ounce lime juice

5 ounces chilled cola

Lime wedge

Combine tequila and lime juice in chilled ice-filled Collins glass. Top with cola; stir until blended. Garnish with lime wedge.

CANTARITO ▶
MAKES 1 SERVING

Lime wedge

Coarse salt

1½ ounces tequila

½ ounce lime juice

½ ounce lemon juice

½ ounce orange juice

Grapefruit soda

Lime, lemon and/or orange wedges

Rub rim of Collins glass with lime wedge; dip in salt. Fill glass with ice; add tequila, lime juice, lemon juice and orange juice. Top with grapefruit soda; stir until blended. Garnish with citrus wedges.

NOTE
In Mexico, Cantaritos are typically served in salt-rimmed clay pots.

MEXICANA
MAKES 1 SERVING

1½ ounces tequila

1½ ounces pineapple juice

1 ounce lime or lemon juice

½ teaspoon grenadine

Fill cocktail shaker with ice; add tequila, pineapple juice, lime juice and grenadine. Shake until blended; strain into ice-filled Collins or highball glass.

ECLIPSE ▶
MAKES 1 SERVING

2 ounces tequila
   añejo

¾ ounce Aperol

¾ ounce cherry
   liqueur

¾ ounce lemon juice

¼ ounce mezcal

   Lemon twist

Fill cocktail shaker with ice; add tequila, Aperol, liqueur, lemon juice and mezcal. Shake until blended; strain into coupe or old fashioned glass. Garnish with lemon twist.

TEQUILA MATADOR
MAKES 1 SERVING

1½ ounces tequila
   blanco (silver)

1 ounce pineapple
   juice

½ ounce lime juice

   Lime or pineapple
   wedge

Fill cocktail shaker with ice; add tequila, pineapple juice and lime juice. Shake until blended; strain into champagne flute or ice-filled old fashioned glass. Garnish with lime wedge.

TEQUILA SUNRISE ▶
MAKES 1 SERVING

2 ounces tequila

6 ounces orange juice (¾ cup)

1 tablespoon grenadine

Place four ice cubes in glass. Pour tequila and orange juice over ice; do not stir. Pour in grenadine; let sink to bottom of glass. (Do not stir.)

MARGARITAS, ALBUQUERQUE STYLE
MAKES 7 TO 8 SERVINGS

1 lime, cut into wedges

Coarse salt

1 can (6 ounces) frozen lime concentrate

¾ cup tequila

6 tablespoons triple sec

1 can (12 ounces) lemon-lime or grapefruit soda

3 to 4 cups ice cubes

Lime twists (optional)

Lime peel (optional)

Rub rim of each cocktail glass with lime wedge; swirl glass in salt to coat rim. Combine half of each of the remaining ingredients, except garnishes, in blender container; blend until ice is finely chopped and mixture is slushy. Pour into salt-rimmed glasses. Repeat with remaining ingredients. Garnish with lime twists and lemon peel.

WHISKEY

Whiskey can also be spelled whisky, without the "e," depending on its country of origin. It is made from three main ingredients—grain, yeast, and water. There are eight variations of whiskey and they each contain their own unique characteristics.

- American whiskey is made from cereal grain mash and is usually light and sweet.
- Bourbon whiskey is made from at least 51% corn. It is flavored with hints of oak, vanilla, and spice.
- Tennessee whiskey is also made from at least 51% corn. It has an oak and vanilla flavor.
- Rye whiskey is made from 51% rye mash with flavors of vanilla, pepper, and coconut.
- Canadian whiskey is made from corn and grain. It has a wide range of flavors, but is usually light and sweet.
- Flavored whiskey varies depending on the ingredients, which range from maple to chocolate.
- Irish whiskey is made from barley. It is usually light and creamy.
- Scotch whiskey is available in different styles, which are made from one or more mixtures of malted barley, wheat, or corn. Flavors include fruit, spice, and vanilla.

◀ Mint Julep (page 94)

SAZERAC ▶
MAKES 1 SERVING

2 ounces whiskey

¼ ounce anise-flavored liqueur

½ ounce simple syrup (recipe follows)

Dash of bitters

Fill cocktail shaker half full with ice; add whiskey, liqueur, simple syrup and bitters. Stir until blended; strain into old fashioned glass.

SIMPLE SYRUP

Bring 1 cup water to a boil; stir in 1 cup sugar. Reduce heat to low; stir constantly until sugar is dissolved. Cool to room temperature; store syrup in glass jar in refrigerator.

MINT JULEP
MAKES 1 SERVING

4 to 6 fresh mint leaves

1 teaspoon sugar

3 ounces bourbon

Sprig fresh mint

Muddle mint leaves and sugar in glass. Fill glass with ice; pour in bourbon. Garnish with mint sprig.

ROB ROY ▸
MAKES 1 SERVING

1½ ounces Scotch or other whiskey

¼ ounce sweet vermouth

Dash of bitters

Maraschino cherry

Fill cocktail shaker half full with ice; add Scotch, vermouth and bitters. Shake until blended; strain into chilled cocktail glass. Garnish with maraschino cherry.

HOT TODDY
MAKES 1 SERVING

Lemon wedge

1 teaspoon honey or sugar

¾ cup hot brewed tea or hot water

1½ ounces whiskey or brandy

Cinnamon stick

Squeeze lemon wedge into warmed mug or Irish coffee glass; stir in honey and drop lemon into glass. Stir in hot tea and whiskey with cinnamon stick.

HUNTER'S COCKTAIL ▶
MAKES 1 SERVING

1½ ounces rye whiskey

½ ounce cherry-flavored brandy

Maraschino cherry

Fill old fashioned glass half full with ice; add whiskey and brandy. Stir until blended; garnish with maraschino cherry.

OLD FASHIONED
MAKES 1 SERVING

1 sugar cube*

2 dashes Angostura bitters

1 teaspoon water

2 ounces whiskey

Lemon peel twist, orange slice and/or maraschino cherry

Or use 2 teaspoons simple syrup (recipe on page 94). Stir together simple syrup, bitters and water in glass.

Place sugar cube, bitters and water in old fashioned glass; muddle until sugar is dissolved. Fill glass half full with ice; stir in whiskey and lemon twist.

RATTLESNAKE ▶
MAKES 1 SERVING

2 ounces whiskey

½ ounce lemon juice

¾ teaspoon powdered sugar

Dash of absinthe or Pernod

1 egg white

Fill cocktail shaker with ice; add whiskey, lemon juice, powdered sugar, absinthe and egg white. Shake until frothy; strain into chilled coupe or cocktail glass.

RUSTY NAIL
MAKES 1 SERVING

1½ ounces Scotch

1 ounce Drambuie

Stir together Scotch and Drambuie in ice-filled old fashioned glass.

DEBONAIR ▶
MAKES 1 SERVING

2½ ounces Scotch or
other whiskey

1 ounce ginger
liqueur

Lemon peel

Fill cocktail shaker half full with ice; add Scotch and liqueur. Shake until blended; strain into chilled cocktail glass. Garnish with lemon peel.

BOILERMAKER
MAKES 1 SERVING

1 ounce whiskey

1 pint beer

Pour whiskey into shot glass. Pour beer into chilled pint glass. Drink whiskey first, followed by beer.

DEPTH CHARGE
Pour 1 ounce whiskey into chilled pint glass; fill with beer.

MANHATTAN ▶
MAKES 1 SERVING

2 ounces whiskey

1 ounce sweet
   vermouth

1 dash Angostura
   bitters

Maraschino cherry

Fill cocktail shaker half full with ice; add whiskey, vermouth and bitters. Stir until blended; strain into chilled cocktail glass or ice-filled old fashioned glass. Garnish with maraschino cherry.

AMBER JACK
MAKES 1 SERVING

2 ounces sweet and
   sour mix

1 ounce Tennessee
   whiskey

½ ounce amaretto

Maraschino cherry

Fill cocktail shaker with ice; add sweet and sour mix, whiskey and amaretto. Shake until blended; strain into chilled cocktail glass. Garnish with maraschino cherry.

BOULEVARDIER ▶

MAKES 1 SERVING

1½ ounces bourbon

1 ounce sweet vermouth

1 ounce Campari

Orange slice or twist

Fill mixing glass or cocktail shaker half full with ice; add bourbon, vermouth and Campari. Stir 30 seconds or until cold; strain into chilled old fashioned or cocktail glass. Garnish with orange slice.

WHISKEY SOUR

MAKES 1 SERVING

2 ounces whiskey

Juice of ½ lemon

1 teaspoon powdered sugar *or* 1 tablespoon simple syrup (recipe on page 94)

Lemon or orange slice and maraschino cherry

Fill cocktail shaker half full with ice; add whiskey, lemon juice and powdered sugar. Shake until blended; strain into ice-filled old fashioned glass. Garnish with lemon slice and maraschino cherry.

VARIATION

Fill cocktail shaker half full with ice; add 4 ounces sweet and sour mix and 1½ ounces whiskey. Shake until blended; strain into ice-filled old fashioned glass. Garnish with lemon slice and maraschino cherry.

SCOFFLAW ▶
MAKES 1 SERVING

1½ ounces rye whiskey	Fill cocktail shaker with ice; add whiskey, vermouth, lemon juice, grenadine and bitters. Shake until blended; strain into chilled coupe or cocktail glass. Garnish with lemon twist.
1 ounce dry vermouth	
¾ ounce lemon juice	
¾ ounce grenadine	
2 dashes orange bitters	
Lemon twist	

IRISH COFFEE
MAKES 1 SERVING

6 ounces freshly brewed strong black coffee	Combine coffee and brown sugar in Irish coffee glass or mug. Stir in whiskey. Pour cream over back of spoon into coffee.
2 teaspoons packed brown sugar	
2 ounces Irish whiskey	
¼ cup whipping cream	

WHISKEY SMASH ▶
MAKES 1 SERVING

2 lemon quarters

8 fresh mint leaves, plus additional for garnish

½ ounce simple syrup (recipe follows)

2 ounces bourbon

Muddle lemon quarters, 8 mint leaves and simple syrup in cocktail shaker. Add bourbon; shake until blended. Strain into old fashioned glass filled with crushed ice; garnish with additional mint.

SIMPLE SYRUP

Bring 1 cup water to a boil; stir in 1 cup sugar. Reduce heat to low; stir constantly until sugar is dissolved. Cool to room temperature; store syrup in glass jar in refrigerator.

GODFATHER
MAKES 1 SERVING

1½ ounces Scotch

½ ounce amaretto

Orange slice or twist

Fill mixing glass or cocktail shaker half full with ice; add Scotch and amaretto. Stir about 20 seconds or until cold; strain into ice-filled old fashioned glass. Garnish with orange slice.

BEER

Following water and tea, beer is one of the oldest and most popular drinks in the world.

Beer is brewed from cereal grains—most commonly from malted barley, although wheat, maize (also known as corn), and rice are also used.

Cider, a longtime staple in Britain, is now growing in popularity possibly as it's a gluten-free alternative to beer.

One of the major differences between beer and cider is their ingredients. While beer is made from malted barley, cider is produced from apple juice.

Ale is a type of beer using a fermentation method that results in a sweet, full-bodied, fruit-flavored taste. Ales are typically darker in color. Lagers tend to be lighter in appearance and are smoother and sweeter to taste.

Stout and porter are dark beers which differ based on the kind of malt used to brew each type. Stouts use unmalted roasted barley, whereas porters use malted barley.

◀ Snake Bite (page 114)

BEER

★ ★ ★ ★ ★

SHANDY ▶
MAKES 1 SERVING

6 ounces chilled beer

6 ounces chilled carbonated lemonade, lemon-lime soda, ginger beer or ginger ale

Lemon slice

Pour beer into chilled large wine glass or pint glass; top with lemonade. Garnish with lemon slice.

SNAKE BITE
MAKES 1 SERVING

8 ounces ale

8 ounces hard cider

Pour ale into chilled pint glass; top with cider. (Do not stir.)

MICHELADA CUBANA
MAKES 1 SERVING

1 lime wedge

Coarse salt

2 tablespoons lime juice

1 teaspoon Worcestershire sauce

1 teaspoon hot pepper sauce

½ teaspoon Maggi seasoning *or* soy sauce

6 ounces chilled Mexican beer (Corona)

Rub rim of beer glass with lime wedge; dip in salt. Fill glass with ice; add lime juice, Worcestershire sauce, hot pepper sauce and Maggi seasoning. Top with beer.

BEER

★ ★ ★ ★ ★

THE CURE ▶
MAKES 1 SERVING

5 ounces light-colored lager

1 ounce ginger liqueur

½ ounce lemon juice

Lemon slices, fresh mint leaves and/ or fresh ginger slices

Fill highball or 12-ounce glass with ice. Add lager, liqueur and lemon juice; stir until blended. Garnish with lemon slices and mint.

BLOODY BEER
MAKES 1 SERVING

Lime wedge (optional)

Coarse salt or celery salt (optional)

3 ounces Bloody Mary mix, tomato juice or tomato-clam juice

1 can or bottle (12 ounces) chilled lager

Rub rim of pint glass with lime wedge; dip in salt, if desired. Pour Bloody Mary mix into glass; top with lager.

BLACK VELVET ▶

MAKES 1 SERVING

3 ounces chilled
   champagne

3 ounces chilled stout

Pour champagne into champagne flute; slowly top with stout.

TIP

For tall glasses, use 4 ounces of each beverage. For pint glasses, use 6 ounces of each.

CIDER SANGRIA

MAKES 4 SERVINGS

1 cup apple cider
   (nonalcoholic)

⅓ cup apple brandy

2 tablespoons lemon
   juice

1 apple, thinly sliced

1 pear, thinly sliced

1 orange, quartered
   and thinly sliced

1 bottle (22 ounces)
   chilled hard cider

Combine apple cider, apple brandy, lemon juice, apple, pear and orange in large pitcher; stir until blended. Just before serving, stir in hard cider. Serve over ice.

HALF-AND-HALF ▶
MAKES 1 SERVING

8 ounces ale 8 ounces porter	Pour ale into chilled pint glass. Pour porter over back of spoon on top of ale. (Do not stir.)

STONE FENCE
MAKES 1 SERVING

2 ounces dark rum, rye or applejack 6 ounces hard cider Lemon twist	Pour rum into pint or old fashioned glass; add 2 to 4 ice cubes. Top with cider; stir until blended. Garnish with lemon twist.

★ ★ ★ ★ ★

WINE & CHAMPAGNE

★ ★ ★ ★ ★

Wine is made from fermented grapes or other fruits. The two most commonly known wine categories are red wines and white wines, but wine can be further broken down into one of seven categories.

- Red wine is made from red or black grapes with grape skins left on throughout fermentation.

- White wine is made by growing and processing white grapes.

- Rosé wine is made from red or black grapes, but grape skins are discarded during fermentation.

- Sparkling wine contains carbon dioxide, which provides its characteristic bubbly quality.

- Sweet wine or dessert wine results from the grapes' naturally occurring sugars that increase the longer the grapes are on the vine.

- Fortified wine has either brandy or another liquer added to it for the purpose of increasing alcoholic content.

- Table wine, usually inexpensive, is meant for everyday use. It is generally a blend of different varieties of grapes. Table wines may be white, red, or rosé.

Champagne is, in fact, a sparkling wine that has gone through a second fermentation in the bottle or cask in which it is sealed.

◀ **Pomegranate Mimosa** *(page 126)*

BUCK'S FIZZ ▶
MAKES 1 SERVING

4 ounces chilled orange juice

2 ounces chilled champagne

½ teaspoon grenadine or cherry liqueur (optional)

Orange wedges (optional)

Pour orange juice into champagne flute; top with champagne. Stir in grenadine, if desired.

POMEGRANATE MIMOSA
MAKES 8 SERVINGS

2 cups chilled pomegranate juice

1 bottle (750 ml) chilled champagne

Pomegranate seeds (optional)

Pour pomegranate juice into eight champagne flutes; top with champagne. Garnish with pomegranate seeds, if desired.

MOONWALK ▶
MAKES 1 SERVING

1 ounce grapefruit juice

1 ounce orange liqueur

3 drops rosewater*

Chilled champagne or sparkling wine

Rosewater can be found at many liquor stores and supermarkets as well as Middle Eastern grocery stores.

Fill cocktail shaker half full with ice; add grapefruit juice, liqueur and rosewater. Shake until blended; strain into champagne flute. Top with champagne.

APEROL SPRITZ
MAKES 1 SERVING

3 ounces Prosecco or sparkling wine

1½ ounces Aperol

Club soda or sparkling water

Orange slice

Fill wine glass or highball glass half full with ice. Add Prosecco, Aperol and splash of club soda; stir gently. Garnish with orange slice.

SHERRY COBBLER ▶
MAKES 1 SERVING

½ teaspoon orange liqueur

½ teaspoon simple syrup (recipe follows)

4 ounces dry sherry (amontillado or oloroso)

Orange slice

Fill large wine glass or old fashioned glass three fourths full with crushed ice; add liqueur and simple syrup. Stir until blended. Gently stir in sherry; garnish with orange slice.

SIMPLE SYRUP

Bring 1 cup water to a boil; stir in 1 cup sugar. Reduce heat to low; stir constantly until sugar is dissolved. Cool to room temperature; store syrup in glass jar in refrigerator.

BLUSHING BRIDE
MAKES 1 SERVING

1 ounce peach schnapps

1 ounce grenadine

4 ounces chilled champagne

Pour schnapps and grenadine into champagne flute; top with champagne. Stir gently until blended.

NELSON'S BLOOD ▶
MAKES 1 SERVING

5 ounces chilled champagne

1 ounce ruby or tawny Port

Pour champagne into champagne flute; top with port. Stir gently until blended.

POINSETTIA
MAKES 1 SERVING

2 ounces cranberry juice

½ ounce orange liqueur

4 ounces chilled Prosecco or champagne

Orange twist

Combine cranberry juice and liqueur in chilled champagne flute; top with Prosecco. Garnish with orange twist.

APPLE CIDER MIMOSA ▶
MAKES 1 SERVING

3 ounces chilled
   apple cider
   (nonalcoholic)
3 ounces chilled
   champagne

Pour cider into champagne flute.
Slowly add champagne; stir gently
until blended.

DIPLOMAT
MAKES 1 SERVING

1½ ounces dry
   vermouth
¾ ounce sweet
   vermouth
¼ teaspoon
   maraschino
   liqueur
Dash orange bitters
Lemon peel

Fill old fashioned glass with ice;
add dry vermouth, sweet vermouth,
liqueur and bitters. Stir until
blended; garnish with lemon peel.

CHAMPAGNE COCKTAIL ▶
MAKES 1 SERVING

1 sugar cube

Dash of bitters

Chilled champagne or dry sparkling wine

Lemon twist

Place sugar cube in chilled champagne flute; sprinkle with bitters. Fill glass with champagne; garnish with lemon twist.

WHITE SANGRIA
MAKES 8 TO 10 SERVINGS

2 oranges, cut into ¼-inch slices

2 lemons, cut into ¼-inch slices

½ cup sugar

2 bottles (750 ml each) dry, fruity white wine (such as Pinot Grigio), chilled

½ cup peach schnapps

3 ripe peaches, pit removed and cut into wedges

2 cups ice cubes (about 16 cubes)

1. Place orange and lemon slices in large punch bowl. Pour sugar over fruit; mash lightly until sugar dissolves and fruit begins to break down.

2. Stir in wine, peach schnapps and peaches; mix well. Refrigerate at least 2 hours or up to 10 hours. Add ice cubes just before serving.

BELLINI ▶
MAKES 1 SERVING

3 ounces peach
nectar*

4 ounces chilled
champagne or
dry sparkling
wine

*Or peel and pit a ripe
medium peach and
purée in blender.*

Pour peach nectar into chilled champagne flute; slowly pour in champagne and stir gently.

MIMOSA
MAKES 1 SERVING

4 ounces cold orange
juice

4 ounces cold
champagne

Orange twist
(optional)

Pour orange juice into champagne flute; top with champagne. Garnish with orange twist.

★ ★ ★ ★ ★

BRANDY

★ ★ ★ ★ ★

Brandy is closely related to wine. The name "brandy" actually comes from the Dutch word "brandewijn" meaning "burnt wine." It is distilled from fruit skins, pulp, and juice. There are three types of brandy including grape, pomace, and fruit.

- Grape brandy is well known. It is produced from grape juice that is double distilled and aged in wooden casks. It is best served at room temperature. Cognac is the most well-known type of grape brandy and is used as the standard for all other types of brandies.

- Pomace brandy is made from pressed grape pulp, skins, and stems after the grapes have been crushed. This brandy is aged in wooden casks and tends to be rather raw.

- Fruit brandy, just like its name suggests, is made from any fruit other than grapes. This type of brandy is usually served chilled or on ice.

◄ Brandy Collins (page 142)

CRANBERRY CAIPIRINHA ▶
MAKES 1 SERVING

2 lime wedges

1 orange wedge

12 fresh cranberries

2 tablespoons brown sugar

2 ounces cachaça

1 ounce cranberry juice

Lime twist or slice

Muddle lime wedges, orange wedge, cranberries and brown sugar in mixing glass or cocktail shaker. Add cachaça and cranberry juice; shake until blended. Strain into ice-filled old fashioned glass; garnish with lime twist.

BRANDY COLLINS
MAKES 1 SERVING

2 ounces brandy

1 ounce lemon juice

1 teaspoon powdered sugar

3 ounces chilled club soda

Orange slice and maraschino cherry

Fill cocktail shaker half full with ice; add brandy, lemon juice and powdered sugar. Shake until blended; strain into ice-filled Collins glass. Add club soda; stir until blended. Garnish with orange slice and maraschino cherry.

VICEROY ▶
MAKES 1 SERVING

1½ ounces pisco
1 ounce Lillet Blanc
½ ounce lime juice
½ ounce simple syrup (recipe follows)
1½ ounces tonic water
Fresh mint sprig

Combine pisco, Lillet Blanc, lime juice and simple syrup in ice-filled highball glass. Top with tonic water; stir gently until blended. Garnish with mint.

SIMPLE SYRUP

Bring 1 cup water to a boil; stir in 1 cup sugar. Reduce heat to low; stir constantly until sugar is dissolved. Cool to room temperature; store syrup in glass jar in refrigerator.

STINGER
MAKES 1 SERVING

2 ounces brandy
¾ ounce white crème de menthe

Fill cocktail shaker half full with ice; add brandy and crème de menthe. Shake until blended; strain into chilled cocktail glass.

JACK ROSE ▶
MAKES 1 SERVING

2 ounces applejack
¾ ounce lime juice
¾ ounce grenadine
Lime slice or wedge

Fill cocktail shaker with ice; add applejack, lime juice and grenadine. Shake about 15 seconds or until cold; strain into chilled cocktail glass or coupe. Garnish with lime slice.

METROPOLITAN
MAKES 1 SERVING

1½ ounces brandy
1½ ounces sweet vermouth
½ teaspoon simple syrup (recipe follows)
Dash bitters
Maraschino cherry

Fill cocktail shaker half full with ice; add brandy, vermouth, simple syrup and bitters. Shake until blended; strain into chilled cocktail glass. Garnish with maraschino cherry.

SIMPLE SYRUP

Bring 1 cup water to a boil; stir in 1 cup sugar. Reduce heat to low; stir constantly until sugar is dissolved. Cool to room temperature; store syrup in glass jar in refrigerator.

CAIPIRINHA ▶
MAKES 1 SERVING

½ lime, cut into wedges

4 teaspoons sugar

2 ounces cachaça*

A Brazilian brandy. Substitute any brandy, if necessary.

Combine lime wedges and sugar in old fashioned glass; muddle with wooden spoon. Fill glass with crushed ice; add cachaça.

CAIPIROSKA

Substitute vodka for cachaça.

CAIPIRISSIMA

Substitute rum for cachaça.

SIDECAR
MAKES 1 SERVING

2 ounces brandy or cognac

2 ounces orange-flavored liqueur

½ ounce lemon juice

Fill cocktail shaker half full with ice; add brandy, liqueur and lemon juice. Shake until blended; strain into chilled cocktail glass.

SANGRIA ▶
MAKES 10 SERVINGS

4 medium oranges, divided

2 lemons, divided

2 bottles (750 ml each) red wine

6 ounces orange-flavored liqueur

3 ounces brandy

⅓ to ½ cup sugar

2 cups cold club soda

1 apple, diced

Juice 3 oranges and 1 lemon; pour juice into punch bowl. Add wine, liqueur, brandy and sugar to taste; mix well to dissolve sugar. Cover and refrigerate 2 to 6 hours. Just before serving, slice remaining orange and lemon. Stir club soda into sangria; add sliced orange, lemon and apple.

VIEUX CARRÉ
MAKES 1 SERVING

¾ ounce cognac

¾ ounce rye whiskey

¾ ounce sweet vermouth

½ teaspoon Benedictine

3 dashes Angostura bitters

Lemon twist

Fill mixing glass or cocktail shaker with ice; add cognac, whiskey, vermouth, Benedictine and bitters. Stir until blended; strain into ice-filled old fashioned glass or cocktail glass. Garnish with lemon twist.

BRANDY ALEXANDER
MAKES 1 SERVING

2 ounces brandy

1 ounce half-and-half

1 ounce dark crème de cacao

¼ teaspoon ground nutmeg

Fill cocktail shaker half full with ice; add brandy, half-and-half and crème de cacao. Shake until blended; strain into cocktail glass. Garnish with nutmeg.

PISCO SOUR
MAKES 1 SERVING

2 ounces pisco

1 ounce lime juice

¼ ounce simple syrup (recipe follows)

½ egg white

1 dash Angostura bitters

Fill cocktail shaker half full with ice; add pisco, lime juice, simple syrup and egg white. Shake until blended; strain into chilled cocktail glass. Sprinkle foam with bitters.

SIMPLE SYRUP

Bring 1 cup water to a boil; stir in 1 cup sugar. Reduce heat to low; stir constantly until sugar is dissolved. Cool to room temperature; store syrup in glass jar in refrigerator.

FRENCH CONNECTION ▶
MAKES 1 SERVING

1½ ounces cognac
¾ ounce amaretto

Fill old fashioned glass three fourths full with ice; add cognac and amaretto. Stir gently until blended.

FRENCH CONNECTION NO. 2:
Substitute orange liqueur for the amaretto.

HOT MULLED CIDER
MAKES 16 SERVINGS

½ gallon apple cider
½ cup packed light brown sugar
1½ teaspoons balsamic or cider vinegar
1 teaspoon vanilla
1 cinnamon stick
6 whole cloves
½ cup applejack or bourbon

Combine apple cider, brown sugar, vinegar, vanilla, cinnamon and cloves in large saucepan; bring to a boil over medium-high heat. Reduce heat to low; simmer 30 minutes. Remove and discard cinnamon stick and cloves. Stir in applejack. Serve warm.

LIQUEUR

Liqueur is the result of infusing liquor, such as brandy or whiskey, with a natural flavoring ingredient, such as fruit, herbs, nuts, and/or cocoa. It is generally served as an after-dinner drink or used as an ingredient in cocktails, cooking, and baking.

Common liqueurs include amaretto (almond), cassis (currant), Cherry Heering (cherry), Cointreau (orange), crème de cacao (chocolate), crème de menthe (mint), Curaçao (orange), Grand Marnier (orange), Kahlúa (coffee), kirsch (cherry), and Triple Sec (orange).

◀ B-52 (page 158)

DON PEDRO
MAKES 1 SERVING

1 cup vanilla ice cream

2 ounces cream

1 ounce whiskey

1 ounce coffee liqueur

Combine ice cream, cream, whiskey and liqueur in blender; blend until smooth. Serve in hurricane glass.

B-52
MAKES 1 SERVING

½ ounce coffee liqueur

½ ounce Irish cream liqueur

½ ounce orange liqueur

Pour coffee liqueur into shot glass; top with Irish cream liqueur, then orange liqueur. (Do not stir.)

GOLDEN DREAM ▶
MAKES 1 SERVING

2 ounces orange liqueur

2 ounces Galliano

2 ounces orange juice

1 ounce whipping cream

Fill cocktail shaker half full with ice; add liqueur, Galliano, orange juice and cream. Shake 30 seconds or until well blended; strain into chilled cocktail glass.

AMARETTO SUNRISE
MAKES 1 SERVING

4 ounces orange juice

1 ounce amaretto

¾ ounce grenadine

Combine orange juice and amaretto in highball or old fashioned glass; stir until blended. Add grenadine; let sink to bottom of glass. (Do not stir.)

LAST WORD ▶
MAKES 1 SERVING

¾ ounce gin

¾ ounce green
    Chartreuse

¾ ounce maraschino
    liqueur

¾ ounce lime juice

Lime twist

Fill cocktail shaker with ice; add gin, Chartreuse, maraschino liqueur and lime juice. Shake until blended; strain into chilled coupe or cocktail glass. Garnish with lime twist.

AMERICANO
MAKES 1 SERVING

1½ ounces sweet
    vermouth

1½ ounces Campari

Chilled club soda

Lemon wedge

Fill glass with ice. Pour vermouth and Campari over ice; fill with club soda. Garnish with lemon wedge.

SWEET RUBY ▶
MAKES 1 SERVING

1 ounce ruby port
¾ ounce amaretto
2 dashes Angostura
   bitters

Fill mixing glass or cocktail shaker with ice; add port, amaretto and bitters. Stir 10 seconds; strain into chilled old fashioned glass half full with ice.

KAMIKAZE
MAKES 1 SERVING

1 ounce vodka
1 ounce triple sec
1 ounce lime juice

Fill cocktail shaker half full with ice; add vodka, triple sec and lime juice. Shake until blended; strain into chilled cocktail glass, large shot glass or ice-filled old fashioned glass.

WHITE LINEN ▶
MAKES 1 SERVING

1½ ounces gin

1 ounce lemon juice

½ ounce elderflower liqueur

½ ounce simple syrup (recipe follows)

Chilled club soda

Fill cocktail shaker with ice; add gin, lemon juice, liqueur and simple syrup. Shake until blended; strain into ice-filled Collins or highball glass. Top with club soda.

SIMPLE SYRUP

Bring 1 cup water to a boil; stir in 1 cup sugar. Reduce heat to low; stir constantly until sugar is dissolved. Cool to room temperature; store syrup in glass jar in refrigerator.

OATMEAL COOKIE COCKTAIL
MAKES 1 SERVING

½ ounce butterscotch schnapps

½ ounce cinnamon schnapps

½ ounce Irish cream liqueur

Pour butterscotch schnapps into shot glass. Pour cinnamon schnapps over back of spoon over butterscotch schnapps. Repeat with Irish cream liqueur. (Do not stir.)

MELON BALL
MAKES 1 SERVING

3 ounces orange or pineapple juice

2 ounces melon-flavored liqueur

1 ounce vodka

Frozen melon balls (optional)

Fill cocktail shaker with ice; add orange juice, liqueur and vodka. Shake until very cold; strain into chilled cocktail glass. Garnish with melon balls.

CAMPARI COOLER
MAKES 1 SERVING

2 ounces orange juice

1 ounce Campari

1 ounce peach schnapps

Juice of 1 lime (about 1½ tablespoons)

Cold club soda or lemon-lime soda

Maraschino cherry and orange wedge

Fill cocktail shaker half full with ice; add orange juice, Campari, peach schnapps and lime juice. Shake until blended; strain into ice-filled margarita or highball glass. Top with a splash of club soda, if desired. Garnish with maraschino cherry and orange wedge.

CHOCOLATE MARTINI ▶

MAKES 1 SERVING

2 ounces vodka or vanilla vodka

1½ ounces crème de cacao

Chocolate shavings and maraschino cherries

Fill cocktail shaker half full with ice; add vodka and crème de cacao. Shake until blended; strain into chilled martini glass. Garnish with chocolate shavings and maraschino cherries.

MINT CHOCOLATE MARTINI

Add ½ ounce crème de menthe to cocktail shaker.

GRASSHOPPER

MAKES 1 SERVING

2 ounces crème de menthe

2 ounces crème de cacao

2 ounces half-and-half or whipping cream

Fill cocktail shaker half full with ice; add liqueurs and half-and-half. Shake until blended; strain into chilled cocktail glass.

MOCKTAILS

Mocktails are simply cocktails that do not contain any alcohol. They include a mix of fruit juices, flavored syrups, and garnishes and can be served as an enjoyable alternative for party guests who prefer not to drink alcohol.

◀ Cucumber Punch *(page 176)*

PINEAPPLE AGUA FRESCA
MAKES 6 SERVINGS

⅓ plus ¼ cup sugar, divided

3 cups fresh pineapple chunks (about ½ of 1 large pineapple)

¼ cup freshly squeezed lime juice

2 tablespoons chopped fresh mint

2 cups club soda, chilled

Ice cubes

Fresh mint sprigs

1. Place ¼ cup sugar in shallow dish. Wet rims of six glasses with damp paper towel; dip rims in sugar.

2. Place pineapple, remaining ⅓ cup sugar, lime juice and chopped mint in blender; blend 30 seconds to 1 minute or until mixture is frothy.

3. Pour into pitcher; stir in club soda. Serve immediately in prepared glasses over ice. Garnish with mint sprigs.

MOCKTAILS

★ ★ ★ ★ ★

SHIRLEY TEMPLE ▶
MAKES 1 SERVING

8 ounces ginger ale
  (1 cup)

1 ounce grenadine

  Lime wedge,
    orange slice
    or maraschino
    cherry

Fill highball glass half full with ice; top with ginger ale and grenadine. Garnish with lime wedge.

CUCUMBER PUNCH
MAKES 10 SERVINGS

1 English cucumber,
  thinly sliced

1 cup water

½ of a 12-ounce
  can thawed
  frozen limeade
  concentrate

1 bottle (1 liter) club
  soda, chilled

  Ice cubes

  Lime wedges
    (optional)

1. Combine cucumber slices, water and limeade concentrate in punch bowl or pitcher. Refrigerate 1 hour.

2. Add club soda and ice just before serving. Pour into glasses. Garnish with lime wedges.

MANGO-LIME VIRGIN MARGARITA

MAKES 2 SERVINGS

2 lime wedges (optional)

2 tablespoons coarse salt (optional)

1 large ripe mango, peeled and cubed (1¼ to 1½ cups)

1 cup ice

½ cup fresh lime juice

⅓ cup water

¼ cup sugar

3 tablespoons orange juice

Lime wedges

1. Rub rims of two margarita glasses with lime wedges; dip in salt, if desired.

2. Combine mango, ice, lime juice, water, sugar and orange juice in blender; blend until smooth. Pour mixture into prepared glasses. Garnish with lime wedges.

GINGER-PINEAPPLE SPRITZER

MAKES 4 SERVINGS

2 cups pineapple juice or cranberry juice

1 tablespoon chopped crystallized ginger

1 cup chilled club soda or sparkling water

Ice cubes

Fresh pineapple wedges and mandarin orange segments (optional)

1. Combine pineapple juice and ginger in small saucepan. Bring to a simmer. Pour into small pitcher. Cover; refrigerate for 8 to 24 hours.

2. Strain juice mixture; discard ginger. Gently stir club soda into juice mixture. Serve in ice-filled glasses. Garnish with pineapple wedges and mandarin orange segments.

WARM AND SPICY FRUIT PUNCH
MAKES ABOUT 14 SERVINGS

4 cinnamon sticks

Juice and peel of 1 orange

1 teaspoon whole allspice

½ teaspoon whole cloves

7 cups water

1 can (12 ounces) frozen cranberry-raspberry juice concentrate, thawed

1 can (6 ounces) frozen lemonade concentrate, thawed

2 cans (5½ ounces each) apricot nectar

SLOW COOKER DIRECTIONS

1. Break cinnamon sticks into pieces. Tie cinnamon sticks, orange peel, allspice and cloves in cheesecloth bag.

2. Combine orange juice, water, juice concentrates and apricot nectar in 4-quart slow cooker; add spice bag. Cover; cook on LOW 5 to 6 hours.

3. Remove and discard spice bag.

CITRUS COOLER

MAKES 9 SERVINGS

2 cups orange juice

2 cups unsweetened pineapple juice

1 teaspoon lemon juice

¾ teaspoon coconut extract

¾ teaspoon vanilla

2 cups cold sparkling water

Ice cubes

1. Combine orange juice, pineapple juice, lemon juice, coconut extract and vanilla in large pitcher; refrigerate until cold.

2. To serve, stir in sparkling water. Serve in ice-filled glasses.

ALMOND JOYFUL MOCKTINI

MAKES 2 SERVINGS

1 tablespoon dark chocolate syrup, plus additional for coating rims of glasses

Shredded coconut

¾ cup original flavor almond milk

¼ cup vanilla coconut milk

3 to 4 ice cubes

1. Coat rims of glasses with syrup; dip in coconut.

2. Combine milks, 1 tablespoon syrup and ice in cocktail shaker. Shake well.

3. Serve chilled in prepared glasses.

INDEX

★ ★ ★ ★ ★

INDEX

★ ★ ★ ★ ★

INDEX

★ ★ ★ ★ ★

INDEX

★ ★ ★ ★ ★

METRIC CONVERSION CHART

★ ★ ★ ★ ★

VOLUME MEASUREMENTS (dry)

$1/8$ teaspoon = 0.5 mL
$1/4$ teaspoon = 1 mL
$1/2$ teaspoon = 2 mL
$3/4$ teaspoon = 4 mL
1 teaspoon = 5 mL
1 tablespoon = 15 mL
2 tablespoons = 30 mL
$1/4$ cup = 60 mL
$1/3$ cup = 75 mL
$1/2$ cup = 125 mL
$2/3$ cup = 150 mL
$3/4$ cup = 175 mL
1 cup = 250 mL
2 cups = 1 pint = 500 mL
3 cups = 750 mL
4 cups = 1 quart = 1 L

VOLUME MEASUREMENTS (fluid)

1 fluid ounce (2 tablespoons) = 30 mL
4 fluid ounces ($1/2$ cup) = 125 mL
8 fluid ounces (1 cup) = 250 mL
12 fluid ounces ($1 1/2$ cups) = 375 mL
16 fluid ounces (2 cups) = 500 mL

WEIGHTS (mass)

$1/2$ ounce = 15 g
1 ounce = 30 g
3 ounces = 90 g
4 ounces = 120 g
8 ounces = 225 g
10 ounces = 285 g
12 ounces = 360 g
16 ounces = 1 pound = 450 g

DIMENSIONS

$1/16$ inch = 2 mm
$1/8$ inch = 3 mm
$1/4$ inch = 6 mm
$1/2$ inch = 1.5 cm
$3/4$ inch = 2 cm
1 inch = 2.5 cm

OVEN TEMPERATURES

250°F = 120°C
275°F = 140°C
300°F = 150°C
325°F = 160°C
350°F = 180°C
375°F = 190°C
400°F = 200°C
425°F = 220°C
450°F = 230°C

BAKING PAN SIZES

Utensil	Size in Inches/Quarts	Metric Volume	Size in Centimeters
Baking or Cake Pan (square or rectangular)	8×8×2	2 L	20×20×5
	9×9×2	2.5 L	23×23×5
	12×8×2	3 L	30×20×5
	13×9×2	3.5 L	33×23×5
Loaf Pan	8×4×3	1.5 L	20×10×7
	9×5×3	2 L	23×13×7
Round Layer Cake Pan	8×1½	1.2 L	20×4
	9×1½	1.5 L	23×4
Pie Plate	8×1¼	750 mL	20×3
	9×1¼	1 L	23×3
Baking Dish or Casserole	1 quart	1 L	—
	1½ quart	1.5 L	—
	2 quart	2 L	—